i am ME

Written, illustrated & designed by Trace Moroney

I am me...
there is no one else
in the whole wide world
who is **exactly** like me...
or exactly like **YOU**!

Even twins – who LOOK exactly the same on the outside – are different from each other on the inside.

They may like or dislike different things,
feel different feelings at different times,
believe in different ideas,
have different thoughts,
and behave in different ways.

These are the things that make each of us **unique**.
(say it: yoo-neek)

Twin A

Likes: carrots, snow, cats, hugs, spiders, playing with friends.
Dislikes: unkind people, sausages, bullies, brussels sprouts.
Believes: the tooth fairy is real.
Sometimes I can be: shy, anxious.
Favourite activity: reading.
I am: thoughtful and kind.

Twin B

Likes: sausages, thunder storms, dogs (especially dachshunds).
Dislikes: broccoli, spiders.
Believes: the world is shaped like a sausage.
Sometimes I can be: grouchy.
Favourite activity: eating sausages.
I am: generous and funny.

I am me... and (most of the time)
I feel good about who I am –
on the inside **and** the outside!

I know that I am not perfect
and don't need to be perfect
to be loved, valued, and accepted
for... just... being... **me**!

Self-esteem is what we think, feel, and believe about ourselves.

Someone who feels good about who they are (most of the time) has **healthy self-esteem**.

Healthy self-esteem is when we think about ourselves in a positive way.

Someone who has healthy self-esteem may believe these things about themselves:

Feels loved and accepted

Feels like they belong

Feels comfortable asking for help

Feels confident

Can make good decisions – ignoring pressure from friends to do otherwise

Feels valued and respected

Finds it easy to make new friends

Can cope with mistakes, failures, or problems by knowing they will get through them and bounce back to their usual self

Often feels good things about themselves

Thinks more good things about themselves than bad things

Feels proud about the things they are good at...

Believes in themselves

and accepts the things they are not so good at

Can stand up for themselves

Having healthy self-esteem doesn't mean you are better than anyone else – but just comfortable and confident being **YOU**.

Someone who feels bad about who they are (most of the time) has **low self-esteem** and may believe these things about themselves:

Does not feel as good as others

Does not like to try new things because they think they won't do them well

Feels uncomfortable playing with others and may prefer to be on their own

Thinks more bad things about themselves than good things

Feels uncomfortable asking for help

Feels as though they do not fit or belong

Feels lonely

Can make bad decisions – and be pressured by friends

Finds it hard to make friends

Thinks more about their mistakes and failures than successes

More likely to be bullied

Having low self-esteem doesn't mean you are worse or not as good as anyone else – but you just ***believe*** that you are.

It is **normal** to go through ups and downs about how you think and feel about yourself.

When you are feeling bad about yourself try to remember the things you like about being you, the things you love... and the things you love to do. Thinking about these good things can help change how you feel!

I am thoughtful and kind and ...

adorable!

I belong

I accept and **respect** my body – on the inside and the outside

I am a really good friend

There are lots of things I love to do

I am loved

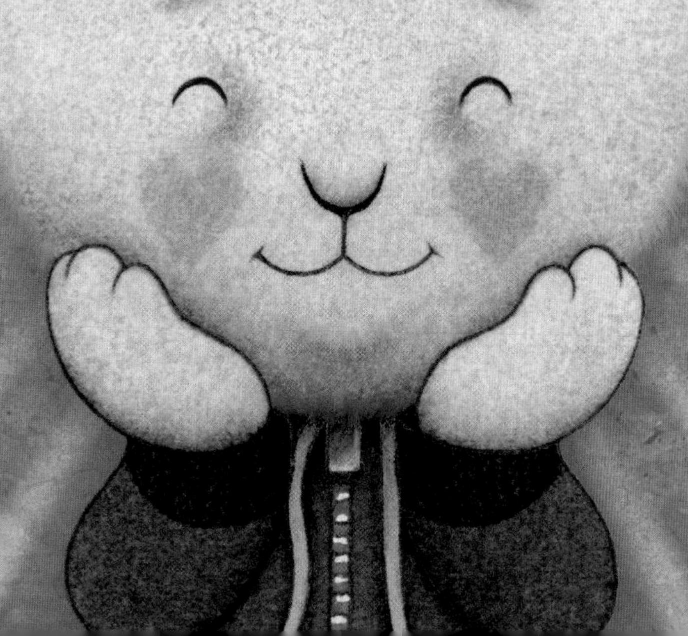

I am ME!

There are lots of things to do to help yourself feel good about who you are – or encourage someone with low self-esteem to try.

Here are 10 ways you can **build** self-esteem:

1. Set a goal

Set a goal and work hard to achieve it – like reading a book (one that is quite hard) all by yourself, running for 10 minutes without stopping, or doing something kind for someone every day.

Start with a small goal, and once you have achieved it – set a bigger one!

Remember: the harder you work to reach your goal the greater the sense of pride and success you feel when you do. Notice how good it feels and how good you feel about yourself!

2. Favourite activities

Write down all the things you love to do – and find ways you can spend more time doing them!

3. Make new friends

Many great friendships start with a simple 'Hello' and a smile!

Some people may not say hello back, but some do!

Try to have a friendly chat about something you may have in common.

4. Join a group or club

Join a group or club that supports your favourite activity.

You will get to meet others who love to do this activity too, and help you feel 'accepted' and a part of a like-minded team.

5. Learn something new

Choose something you would like to learn about or how to do – like playing a musical instrument, swimming, art, or computer skills.

Some parts may be really hard and some may be easy – but say to yourself: 'I am going to ENJOY every part of this new experience.'

6. Be kind to others

Find ways to help others, do something nice for someone, or give someone a compliment like 'You are a really good friend' or 'You have a lovely smile.'

7. Be kind to yourself

It is NORMAL to fail at some things and make mistakes. Life is not a success-only journey! In other words, accept there will be some things you will be good at and some things you will be not so good at ... and it's OK!

Learn to laugh at yourself when you make a silly mistake.

8. Ask for help

Ask someone for help if you need it. It can be to help you achieve a goal, sort out a problem, or to get some advice or support.

9. Talk with someone

Talking about a problem, or your thoughts and feelings, with someone you trust can help take the pressure off – and help you understand that you don't have to cope with everything on your own.

10. Write a list

Write a list of all the things you like about yourself AND the things you really love to do. Find ways you can spend more time being and doing these things each day.

Focus on your strengths and the things you LOVE!

I am **me**... and I don't want to be someone else or pretend to be someone else... because that would be a waste of all the amazing things that make me uniquely **me**!

I am ME.

self-
esteem

ACTIVITY: FOCUS ON THE GOOD STUFF!

Using a pencil (so you can rub out or change if you want to) tick the red ♥✓ hearts that use words that **YOU** think best describe **YOU**. Then tick the orange ♥✓ hearts that describe things you would ***like to be*** – or would like to be more of.

Remember to be realistic and fair to yourself – this activity is just for **YOU**! Ask a grown-up to explain what some of these words mean if you need help.

My name is .... and I am .... years old.

The date is: .... day of .... (month) 20........ (year).

I am...

♥ ♥ KIND	♥ ♥ RESILIENT
♥ ♥ RESPECTFUL	♥ ♥ POLITE
♥ ♥ CURIOUS	♥ ♥ GENTLE
♥ ♥ GENEROUS	♥ ♥ ACCEPTING
♥ ♥ FRIENDLY	♥ ♥ LOVING
♥ ♥ TRUSTWORTHY	♥ ♥ HONEST
♥ ♥ THOUGHTFUL	♥ ♥ FUNNY
♥ ♥ RELIABLE	♥ ♥ LOYAL

CONSIDERATE

GRATEFUL

ENTHUSIASTIC

SENSITIVE

PEACEFUL

HONEST

OPTIMISTIC

CONFIDENT

LOVABLE

CARING

FORGIVING

✓ UNIQUELY ME!

Other things I like about me: ....

....

....

Things I love doing: ....

....

....

....

....

Now, find ways you can **do** and **be** more of these things throughout every day! This is a great activity for grown-ups who are working on self-esteem too.

NOTES TO PARENTS AND CAREGIVERS

Most of us believe we have an understanding of the term **self-esteem**, but how many of us have considered the profound effect that having healthy self-esteem – or low self-esteem – has on our lives? And, more importantly, how do we instill, grow, and nuture healthy self-esteem in our children?

***Self-esteem** is what a person thinks, feels, and believes about themselves – a sort of measure of how much they value and like who they are.*

Self-esteem starts to develop as early as infancy, beginning with either attentive, loving, and positive care – or indifferent, dismissive, or neglectful care – by the parent. While there is still much to be learned and understood about self-esteem, the following factors are believed to be of influence: reactions of others, age, thoughts, social circumstances, genetics, personality, health, life experiences, and comparing self to others.

Self-esteem plays an essential role in our children's academic achievement, engagement in activities, relationships with others, willingness to participate, sense of wellbeing, resilience, and their ability to manage life's inevitable ups and downs in a healthy way.

Children with healthy self-esteem are more resilient (able to bounce back from failure, disappointment, or challenges); feel secure in building and maintaining authentic, healthy relationships; are less critical of themselves and others; are better able to manage stress; are comfortable with independent activity and trying new things; feel a sense of belonging; feel confident to make good decisions; feel confident and comfortable expressing feelings, wants, and needs; and enjoy an increased sense of wellbeing.

Conversely, children with low self-esteem frequently feel negative emotions such as sadness, fear, frustration, anxiety, depression, or ***worthlessness***; are easily irritated or angered; find it difficult to maintain relationships; avoid trying new things or quit early; ***never feel good enough***; are highly critical of themselves and their abilities; doubtful about their decision making; focus on their weaknesses; and find it difficult to express feelings, wants, and needs.
And research indicates low self-esteem is linked to antisocial behaviour, violence, substance abuse, eating disorders, and suicide.

The good news is self-esteem is not fixed – it can be changed, shaped, and improved upon, regardless of age. Not only can you build or improve your own self-esteem, but you have a crucial role in fostering healthy self-esteem in your child.

So ... "how do I go about doing this?" you may ask. Here are 10 simple ways you can help grow your child's self-esteem ...

Be a good role model. Your child will learn to model the behaviours they observe in you – the way you talk about yourself and others; how you engage in activities; and set and achieve (or not) your goals. *Never use harsh name-calling* – as it can become a harmful label a child learns to believe about themselves.

Focus on strengths. Create opportunities (every day) for your child to *do* and *be* more of the things they enjoy and are good at. Focusing more on strengths rather than weaknesses helps your child feel good about who they are.

Set goals. Keep expectations realistic and start with small goals. Remember to praise progress and effort, and model and encourage mindfulness (i.e. engagement in an activity). The harder the effort = a greater sense of pride and success when a goal is achieved.

Be a soft place to fall. In other words, actively listen to your child's thoughts, feelings, and concerns *without criticism or judgement*. Encourage your child to come up with possible solutions to a problem (or brainstorm together), and discuss potential outcomes together.
Earn your child's trust so they will feel comfortable coming to you with any future problem.

Create a sense of belonging. A child who feels as though they belong, are included, or accepted has a greater sense of security and confidence, and feels better supported to handle difficulties.

Learn and try new things. Challenge your child to try something new every day (or do this together) – it could be trying a new food, a new activity, or trying out a new response or behaviour. Keep a record, as it is fun to look back on all the new things you have experienced.

Foster love. Reinforce that your child is *unconditionally loved and valued* for who they are. Don't assume your child knows that you love them, so it is important to explicitly tell them – and why (e.g. by describing some endearing attributes you have observed and appreciate).

Freedom of control. With your guidance and support, allow your child a greater sense of control, allow them to make age-appropriate decisions and mistakes *without criticism*, and discuss learning opportunities. It is equally important to acknowledge and discuss their successes – their sense of achievement in their effort, decision making, or a job well done.

Do not compare with others. Encourage your child to *not* compare themselves to others. Altered or false imagery is prolific on social media platforms, TV, and other mediums, and many people fall victim to these grossly manufactured and manipulated 'ideals' – making us feel less than or not as successful.

Frequently remind your child they are loved and valued for simply being their beautiful and unique self!

For more information and support material visit: **www.tracemoroney.com**

To be yourself in a world that is constantly
trying to make you something else
is the greatest accomplishment.

Ralph Waldo Emerson

Published with love by EQ Publications Ltd
email: hello@eqpublications.nz

www.tracemoroney.com
Edited by Madeleine Collinge

Printed in China by
RR Donnelley Asia Printing Solutions Ltd.

First published 2022.

Hello! I'm Trace Moroney.

I create books about big feelings for little people ... and I absolutely **LOVE** every part of the process.

Through extensive research, carefully chosen words, thoughtful design and illustrations, and a whole bunch of passion, I translate complex emotions for young children and their families.

I am bursting with excitement about this ground-breaking new series created to help equip our children with valuable skills to navigate their way through life's ups and downs.

Wishing you much love and happiness,
Trace
xox